Chocolate Che

Also by Damian Furniss

The Duchess of Kalighat

Damian Furniss

Chocolate Che

Shearsman Books
Exeter

Published in the United Kingdom in 2010 by
Shearsman Books Ltd
58 Velwell Road
Exeter EX4 4LD

ISBN 978-1-84861-106-1
First Edition

Acknowledgements
are due to the editors of the following publications:
*Aesthetica, City Lighthouse, Dog, Fire River, Flying Post, Headlock, The Journal,
Odyssey, Orbis, Ore, Popshot, Shearsman, Smith's Knoll, South, Spectrum, Stand,
Staple, Tears in the Fence, Terrible Work, Tremblestone.*

Versions of some of these poems first appeared in the chapbook *The Duchess
of Kalighat*, published by Tears in the Fence, after winning their pamphlet
competition.

Thanks also to the Fire River Poets, the Mincing Poets, Uncut Poets and Phil
Bowen for their support and encouragement.

The following artists feature in, are the inspiration for, or the voices of,
some of the poems in 'My White Ghosts': Jackson Pollock, Henri Matisse, Pablo
Picasso, Paul Gauguin, Vincent van Gogh, Francis Bacon, Amedeo Modigliani,
Jeanne Hébuterne, Lucian Freud, Balthus, Marc Chagall, Egon Schiele,
Salvador and Gala Dalí, James McNeill Whistler, Edward Hopper, Andy Warhol,
Tracey Emin, Damien Hirst, Gilbert and George, Alfred Wallis
and Mark Rothko.

CONTENTS

Return to Kalighat

Chocolate Che

Chocolate Che

To celebrate Thanksgiving Day
The Yankees baked a chocolate Che
With buttermilk from Camaguey
And cacao from the factory
He founded in the heady days
When cocoa was revolutionary.

He wore a marzipan beret,
Its insignia that rarity—
A perfect star-shaped strawberry—
To strip the comandante
Who took the I from industry
Of the badge that gave him dignity.

They gagged him with a Cadbury's flake
Imported by the C.I.A.
And stretched him on a rack of cane
Lashed onto a Chevrolet,
Carved him up at Gitmo Bay
With harvest blunt machetes—

Took his head to the Admiralty
As their cut of the bounty
That is *La Isla Grande*,
Then toasted him with rum flambé
In memory of Hemingway—
Red flames, like the blues, they fade away

Three Buckets for Love

Welcome to my home. I do not live here.
This is the bathroom, it has no bath.
Three buckets for love, a dripping tap.

Frames without doors, the curtains part—
Mama launders bread in her chamber pot.
Welcome to my home, she does not live here.

Her vest bares a rash of day-glo hearts.
Under the arc of a hung bulb stand
Three buckets for love. A dripping tap

Ticks stage left of our netted bed.
Brothers call cues from the room next door.
Welcome to my home, they do not live here.

Papa stirs the pot, tucks in with his spoon—
A black bean soup with bones, twice stewed—
Three buckets for love. A dripping tap

Salutes the dawn. Stool pigeons perch behind
The moon. Two parrots rap on the washing line.
Welcome to my home. You do not live here.
Three buckets for love. A dripping tap.

The Existentialist Sandwich

I order a sandwich—
A dairy-free sandwich
A meatless, vegless sandwich
Plain as a Ukrainian
Sliced bread naked
As the day it was baked

My waiter, the doctor
The doctor, my waiter
Pleads to authority
The rule of ledgers
Dictates equal measures
Of ham and cheese

A Spaniard intervenes
Declares an open sandwich
Curdled milk and meat
Untainted by wheat
Gherkins on the side—
A Spaniard's dream

We split the sandwich
Like a breast man, a leg man
Might share a striptease
Order Daiquiris
To celebrate the victory
Of west over east

While the waiter dreams of sandwiches—
The imaginary sandwich
The sandwich that makes itself
The sandwich that eats other sandwiches
For breakfast, lunch and dinner
The sandwich that just wants to be.

My Daddy Was a Studebaker

In the era of General Motors, on a day in late September, we left
Detroit: headed due south, chrome noses sniffing at the moon.

We were of twelve marques. There were the Cadillacs and the
Chevrolets; the Plymouths, the Buicks and the Pontiacs. But my
Daddy was a Studebaker. Built like an airplane, he yearned to fly.

We travelled in convoy, followed the migration routes from the
Windy City down to Miami. We had sitting rooms inside us and ate
at roadside diners. Gas was cheaper than water then—we just stuck a
long straw into the earth and sucked up its blood.

At the ocean's edge we greased our trunks with pomade and primed
our fins for the sea. By the power of Henry Ford, the waves parted.
We sounded our horns as we passed the Florida Keys, said goodbye to
the Land of the Free.

Havana was just a short cruise away. Life was good those first days of
be-bop, mojitos, and cabaret. We were always well lubricated. Our
parts replaced themselves. On rest days, a valet rubbed us down.

But then, without warning, we were abandoned on the runway.
Horses descended from the mountains. Beards sprouted from pencil
thin moustaches. From that day on, time was a cinema reel.

Only rumours from our homeland kept us going, our tyres bald but
unbroken. New marques had crossed the ocean, invading the ports of
our kin. All signs pointed east and we followed them, eight lanes of
asphalt ending in a field.

Not used to hard labour, we drank sugar cane, spluttered and grew
weak. In the city, our cousins married Russians, had their hearts
transplanted for Ladas.

Now we're rented out for weddings or made to escort tourists. Hitchers show us their onions. When strangers stroke our bonnets, we blow smoke into their faces.

But my Daddy was a Studebaker. I was made an American, with American dreams. There are roles in the movies for cars like me.

(This Sonnet Is Sponsored By) Sonneti

Dig the dirt, Henry. Sift for dead men's teeth.
Yank steak and kidney from that big cat's jaw.
Pluck blood fruit, Henry, from the citrus trees,
Snatch back your heart, a beat between the claws
Of feline Fidel, with his snake-hipped grin
Spitting pips of morse, launching nicotine
From the face that launched a thousand cigars
With a mundungus broadcast of catarrh.

My time is yours, Henry—our time, not his.
His time is through now, worn like faded fatigues.
No one told you, Henry, there'd be days like this—
Pulling Che poses in your Sonneti jeans.
Tug your cap down, Henry. If the dead could speak
They'd take the long knives to your radical chic.

Goodfella

Spain is fine this time of year
But a deckchair is no place
For such a great buffoon.
Why, he said grace with men
Cut from every cloth, hung
Their hats and heads from hooks.

Now he goes to bed at dawn
To drink a case of sun, dreaming
Of the night the stage was his—
A balcony of stars twinkled
With applause, wise guys roared
For blood, rained down the fizz.

But old man moon will rise again
In spats, a cane and monocle,
Barking through the curtains like a loon.
Red cheeked and open mouthed
He bore his glorious behind
For the glad eyes in the crowd—

They say the songs he sung
Cast sequins on the hides
Of each diva in the chorus line
As he climbed the spiral stairway,
His top hat and a bren gun
All we have to remember him by.

Che in Disguise

Plucked bald as a yam,
Grey streaked in the minge
That remains of his mane,
Che snipes off two frames,
Puffs in the desk-weight
That strains at his waist.
Fat cat that ran a bank
Wants to play at mouse
In a mask of Bakelite
He buffs up, checks twice—
Fails to recognise himself.

His wife herds in the kids,
Geese who poke and hiss
At each other, then notice
The silver fox, thoughtful
In the corner. He takes each
To his gurning mouth,
Shoos them squealing out.
His daughter pouts bye-byes,
Tells her anxious mother
That Uncle she'd not met
Just fell in love with her.

Fidel's Beard

Fidel's beard is a little explored region beneath Fidel's nose. A jungle once exposed to Agent Orange, Napalm and carpet-bombing, reports the area is still subject to a secret war have been confirmed by satellite photographs that show its coverage is less lustrous than before, although some claim it is merely a victim of climate change, being much ravaged by hurricanes.

Fidel's beard has been serenaded by barbershop quartets in the pay of the CIA. Long admired by mothers with combs and handkerchiefs, all the double agents sent to massage its host with DDT switched their defoliant for talcum powder and joined the beard's secret harem. But now, insiders say, the beard of our former enemy is little more than a flea circus, its tick acrobats turning tricks for visiting dignitaries.

Fidel's beard has tickled more muchachas than the sproutings of Marx or Lenin. Scrapbooks of its cuttings fill several miles of library shelving. Over fifty years in the growing, it has received more decorations than any other beard in history. It has outlasted nine beardless American presidents. Not so much as a single moustache has been grown against it. But all these words say no more than the stroking of a chin conveys.

Havana's the Woman

Havana's the woman I long for:
Her gap-toothed smile an open door
From my world into hers, clothes hung
From her balcony, flags of welcoming
As I rumba up the Malecon
A suitcase of shoes under my arm
Just to hear the cha-cha-cha
Of her heels as she greets me
With an invitation to *bailar.*
Kick off your crocodile shoes, she'll say,
And mambo like Benny Moré.

And though she is no longer young
The trill song of her laugh will fill
Our garden with the tra-la-la
Of a lovebird, still an old fifteen.
And when we marry, her family
Will deck our Cadillac with lilies,
Then pelt me with rice and beans.
And when I leave her, forms in hand,
She'll rock her chair against the sea
As waves crash over the harbour wall
And then retreat into history.

Woodpecker Blues

I left the woodpecker on Carpentier's grave.
It was no accident. Some tomcat gave
Me a feathered gift. Be warned,
That knocking bird was surely born
To die—one tug of my string garrotte
And the bird that was, was not.

I left the woodpecker by Carpentier's tomb.
I swept up lesser birds to make room
For that artisan of the woodland sky.
Your Honour, I'm guilty, I cannot lie—
To give this poem its wry punch line,
I took that chiseller in his prime.

I left the woodpecker in Carpentier's bed.
There he sleeps between sheets of lead
With a stone Chihuahua at his feet,
A marble bone between her teeth.
This is my tribute to the great creator
Who's gone to earth to meet his maker.

I left the woodpecker where Carpentier rests.
A man asleep is a man twice blessed:
To dream of death and then awake
Are the habits that a writer make
And Alejo gave birth to other worlds
Where page is sky and words are birds.

See That My Bones Are Kept Clean

When I go, polish my bones:
Rub them down with alcohol
And drink the dregs of rum
From a glass half-full
Now that mine is fully empty.
Lay down your half-cocked guns,
Sharpen your sharpest knives
And scriven your poems on me.

Grease up your jazz trombones
(I know, you don't like jazz)
And wear your gladdest rags
(Leave your sober suits at home.)
If you never learned to dance,
Now's the time to learn to dance.
(If you still fear old Jim Crow
Then leave those fears at home.)

Do you play the saxophone?
(I don't play the saxophone.)
Alto, tenor, bass—whatever—
Bring all your horns along,
Just play your favourite song
(Each in turn, all together)
Stormy Fruit or Strange Weather,
My cadaver will sing along.

When I'm gone, do not moan
On my long, unbroken bones
But chink your ringed fingers
On tumblers well slung
With slugs of darkest rum—
Cut loose among the royal palms,
Your longest cigars lit from
The flame of Cuba libre.

Semana Santa

On Palm Sunday a gypsy reads my hand. The life-line is short, the love-line broken.

On Monday we work. Mondays are never holy, though sometimes they are holidays.

On Shrove Tuesday we'd eat pancakes. But there are no pancakes. And it isn't Shrove Tuesday.

On Wednesday the volcano erupts. Sometimes it snows in April. Other times, it hails fire and brimstone.

On Maundy Thursday we offer to bathe the feet of passers-by. We reel around the fountain all day. No one volunteers.

On Good Friday the white men play Christ, the Indians Romans. For the rest of the year their roles are reversed.

On Saturday, we watch a soccer match while Jesus and his disciples take a rest. A priest blesses the ball. It's a no score draw.

On Easter Sunday we follow a trail of rose petals up to the crosses on the hill; the three of them still hang there like bats.

On Monday we go home disappointed. Another year without a miracle.

Playing Bones

Put to bed with flesh,
Naked, they rise
White as milk teeth,
White as your eyes.

It takes a small child
To sort men from boys
Scraping with his knife,
Shaping bones into toys

This one is a tank
And this is its gun—
A clean split skull,
The shaft of his thumb;

These are the bombs
Of a bone winged plane—
Disjointed fingers,
Chipped vertebrae

And these were the ribs
Of another small boy—
His unbroken cage
Is a musical toy

You play with a bone
That shivers as it taps,
It's warm in the fist
And cold when it snaps.

A Time for Gifts

It was a bus to shake
the finger cymbals
off a Creole tambourine.

Maria shielded her dumpy breast
with the brow of a bowler hat,
her baby suckling, concealed
amongst many skirts and blouses.

Lips wrapped round a husk of corn,
she played a mean blues harp, spat
bad chunks out with broken teeth.
I unwrapped a slab of Cadbury's,

laid some on my tongue. She gripped
my hand with knitting fingers,
motioned to that stumpy mouth.
I endorsed toothpaste with a smile,

gave her my second, still sealed bar.
It disappeared into folds of shawl.
A sleight of hand—warming on my palm
the gift of an embalmed hummingbird:

soft as vicuña fleece,
the blue of azurite;
rare as love.

Pisco Sour

That day, we'd watched llamas breed. 'The quim of the female is the closest to the human of any animal I've seen,' she said. Not knowing many, I couldn't comment.

That night, we listened to a Quechuan band play Paul Simon tunes on ukuleles and pan pipes. 'Do you like folk music?' I asked. She drummed with her fingers.

'Let's go back to the hotel,' she said. 'Play cards and quaff some more.' I didn't hang around, downed my lemonade in one.

We drank her Pisco Sour, just a dip of sugar to coat the rim. Then we played our hands. I'd taught boys at a school run by monks. She'd been an intern at a Chilean clap clinic. She won.

'Twenty-eight dicks in one day, dripping slime and sore with strains of VD not yet medically identified—I never want to screw again!'

My stories of days in class did not impress. Soon, she went to bed, while I slept on the rug. In Santiago, someone she had touched touched someone else. We sighed.

Arequipa Rain

Arequipa rain fell sharp,
slashed the sky apart;
needling the earth
at its swollen heart;
exposing ragged seams
across its tapestry.

Streets went walkabout,
barrios relocated; shacks
inside out, pylons castrated;
pipes gaping, disconnected;
a drought in time of flood.

All roads but one water-plugged,
we gringos bought safe passage
to Mollendo, a bikini beach
where waters break on Atacama's bones.

In the sluiced hills
they fought to fill buckets
from the swollen Rio Chilli—
a dozen drowned.

On the raked sands
we sought to limit burns
with Andean umbrellas—
and baked deep brown.

Noah on the ark, sunbathing:
all the time in the world—
and none of its cares.

Bee Movie

Edith—
A pigtail-threaded hat,
Face like a shaven cat,
Eyes of charcoal, burning.

Elva—
Lean as a guinea pig,
More skirts than a whirligig,
Scarlet poncho, twirling.

Caleb—
Back broadened by dung sacks,
Nose sharp as a chopping axe,
A cup of hands, shaking

Sense from the heads of bees
That nimble fingers noose with thread
And harness to a red balloon;
The sun hauled off by circus fleas

To float above the village square.
From here, a golden butterfly
And just as brief, it disappears;
A breath in mountain air.

Edith—
Dead as a wedding goat,
Smile drawn across her throat,
Mouth stuffed with hair.

Elva—
Eyes bunged with Pisco corks,
Skirts pinned by pitchforks,
Thighs torn by a bear.

Caleb—
Holes in his jungle boots,
Dug in like potato root,
Mumbling a prayer.

Hot Water

We watched the sun rise over Macchu Picchu in handcuffs. That'll teach us, hiking without a permit.

The first night, we'd eaten guinea pig and slept in a pigsty.

The second night, our tents were slit from head to foot; some of us lost our porridge, others their passports.

But there was something about us the cops liked. They were fat, short and hairy. We were thin, tall and blonde. They were dirty old men. We weren't.

They let us free on the promise of bad behaviour. We suffered a night at the springs; the girls bounced on their laps while us boys poured them beer. They had the time of their lives.

Cheaper than a bribe, we joked. We should've known the quiet one spoke English.

He translated the name of the town for us: *Hot Waters*.

Next day, they returned us to where we were found, our wallets empty as their smiles.

Dog Town

Once there were people here.
Then, no people—only dogs.

Guerrillas moved in. Painted
their slogans. Moved out, red-handed.

Soldiers moved in. Whitewashed
the walls. Withdrew, pale-faced.

When the army killed a guerrilla
they fed him to the dogs.

When the guerrillas killed a soldier
they fed him to the dogs.

The dogs didn't take sides.
They ate what they were given.

'Murder is meat' they barked,
growing fat and content.

There were dogs here,
then there were no dogs—

They hung from the lampposts,
blinking, like unexploded bombs.

Yungay

I

Another shift of pain.
Huascaran creaks in her discomfort.
Her belly is full now—
she is fit to burst.

The earth rolls in labour—
her moans resound from peak to peak,
quaking the thin floor
of existence, shaking the world.

When her turquoise waters break
amniotic fluid pours—an avalanche
of alluvium guts the valley in a trance
of eighteen thousand open mouths.

II

The scree skin is a membrane
that contains a nation's scream.
I am walking on the rooftops—
flowers don't grow, are left
in this Gethsemane, grave bouquets.

I nod to Christ, statued on the high ground.
His white arms are open to the world.
My eyes meet his, and mine flinch.

Below, a church spire sticks its steel finger
through the sterile dust. Crosses stab the crust
of earth, that is these fields, that were a town.

How do the few know
where those who never woke
lay, six or sixteen feet below?
Truth is, they don't.

The bus driver sounds his horn to go.
We shift like smoke, as tourists do.

Mummies

The mummies in the desert are not pretty. They grin inanely, like maiden aunts left buried at the beach.

Our taxi-guide is stubby as a mechanic's unwashed thumb.

'Take off your clothes,' he says, thrusting a gun into my back. 'And then take off hers.'

He has her tie me while he watches. Then he ties her while I watch.

He sniffs our clothes as he shakes them down, and then drives away, kicking sand into our faces.

By the time our rescuers come, we are well done.

For three weeks, we sit outside the Embassy with signs round our necks saying 'we have nothing.'

Shoeshine boys drop coins into our paper cups.

Third Hand

Rosa works the bar
with single cigarettes,
a packet of ten
noosed round her neck.

She moves to distract
white men from drink,
mimes with her mouth
the pleasures of smoke.

*I could smack that kid
like an egg,* one says.
She's good enough to eat.

*Patience will roll
a cigar on those thighs,*
the other replies.
She'll blow a devil's ring.

A third licks a note,
still stippled with coke,
and pays her to sing.

Her hand clasps the ghost
of a knife. Blood in her glance,
on her feet. Her dance
makes three hands of two;
she winks as she strikes.

In the morning they find
themselves a gram light
and rub down their skin
like mad men convinced
they've been shaved in the night.

The Cola War

Uncle Paco rose from his grave
on The Day of the Dead
complaining the cola we sprayed
on the stone at its head
had tickled his tongue
with the taste of honey gone bad—

not his chosen brand.

The litter of tops proved as much—
one was wrongly embossed—
so he took the bottle in hand
broke its neck on a rock
and gouged a hole in the boss
of the gaseosa stand
until his siphon spewed red—

the Cola War had begun.

Shock troops arrived
in pickup trucks, stencilled
stucco in blue or red.
Bullets danced to
their sponsor's tune,
jingled on hot tin roofs—

feuds played out beneath signs.

And Paco says
the first soda, red or blue,
to land its logo on the moon,
that side has won—

until then, the battle goes on.

The Orchid Collector

The old man scours the rainforest for specimens, grafts them to the grove of his jungle home. Each new species, flowers flow through his pen onto the page, are mailed away to the universities of the world.

He names each after one of his children, catalogues them into history. 'This is your flower,' he tells them when they are old enough to care. 'This is how the world knows who you are.'

And though, if pulled straight, he is tall with skin as white as his hair, his wives are brown and small. He cares for them as they do for him, each in their different ways.

He does not drink often, but when he does he retreats to his room, dismantles his pistol, cleans and reassembles it, then tests its mechanism by firing a shot.

When he is satisfied, he polishes the swastika engraved into its handle, smiling to himself. He has led a good life. He has had many offspring: each of his beauties has blue eyes; some of them are blonde.

A Dormitory Between Us

Was it the third bed or the fourth
you took me in, teeth like a puma
tearing flesh from the moon,
or a shark peeling a seal?

I know we slept in the fifth
in an exhausted pool
without a swab of sheet
to keep us from its coils,
spiralling into sin.

On the first, we had talked
of love without promises
and life without daylight—
the conversation was short.

By the second, you undressed
us both, a hand for each clasp,
button, zipper or belt.
I saw the mystery of Peru—
pearls in a purse made of felt.

When I awoke, it was as if
I'd been savaged by a dream—
alone in that room, the undead
cockroaches roused by dawn,
and you, my little vampire, departed

like a flood. Alone, six sad beds
and each bore a slick of you—
sugar cane pap, anchovy sweat—
the one we had not touched
smudged with a fur of blood.

The Art Hotel

At the Art Hotel, the waiters are painters, the bartenders actors, and the chefs conductors.

The maid and I are sculptors; we share our innermost thoughts in the exchange of sculptures made of towels.

She glides a white swan across my single, wan duvet. It speaks to me of the age of chivalry and romance

I commit an abstract design to the floor, damp and soiled as what a former lover once called my soul.

The next day, the maid creates a peacock, its tail a fan of blue and green bath sheets, its comb a crimped flannel.

I build a towelling tower for her, almost as tall and sour as what that same ex-lover told me I can sometimes be.

On the day I am due to leave, I discover her making a towel moulding of herself, her hot little body wrapped up like an Egyptian mummy.

We collapse in a pile of towels. Soap and water are just the start of it. I have never felt so clean, so refreshed.

Then I catch sight of an invoice in her own hand, addressed to me, a dollar a day for sculptures rendered.

A work of art is an act of love, I say, and only the artist should pay the price for it.

The maid eats the towels on which we lay and I applaud her wit.

Che's Hands

Che's grave is not Che's grave.
And the bones in it are not Che's.
And those cold hands in the jar
tucked away in Fidel's pantry—
they are not the hands of Che,
though they are both human
and Che-like. And that wax mask
that impressed the face of Che
did not impress the face of Che.
And those photos of the dead Che
as Christ, with the generals playing
Romans, display neither Christ,
nor Che, nor Romans. And his wounds
are not wounds as we know them.
And all the tales of Che you've read
are not tales with Che in them.
And all these Che poems are not
Che poems, or even poems at all.
And if you took a lock of the hair
of Che, it is Che's hair no longer.
And if you say that Che was a saint,
you either did not meet that Che
or you have never met a saint.
And any likeness at all between
my Che and your Che is coincidental,
if you believe in coincidence,
which Che did not. And if you say
Che lives, then Che lives, although
he doesn't live, and isn't Che.
And if I say Che never lived, then that
is all I have to say about Che.

My White Ghosts

My White Ghosts

Where have my white ghosts been?
Busy in other men's dreams, I suppose

Or at repose on their white sheets
Like watermarks hiding from sun.

With their white lips, white eyes
And white hair you'll recognise them

Drawing lots for a night in my head,
Splitting straws over whose turn to lose

And who's to win that sleep in the dark
Where being ghostly means something.

So where have my white ghosts gone?
Wherever I shine my bright beam

There are just shadows, or dogs
Pretending to be white. Please God

Send my white ghosts home tonight,
I've a party planned for Halloween—

My white ghosts will drink and smoke
Before writing new poems for me.

Then they'll be seen floating away
And hooting most hauntingly.

If Art Was a Car

If art was a car, I'd take this line for a spin
Round the east fork of Long Island in deep summer
From bar to bar, woman to woman, half a bourbon

Between my thighs, making one curve then another,
Swivelling a circle just because I can—
Now that would be a day, a day worth living.

But art is not a car, and to drive is not to paint
As James Dean or Baby Jayne would surely testify
If their bodies were those of cars that could be fixed.

Or my own uncle, the butcher, chauffeured down the A46
Hand waving out the window, a bleeding finger in its fist,
Then a year later, taking the wall of dawn head on

Like Pollock took on art when the canvas was still empty
As a salt flat in the sun, and the world was young
As my uncle, who didn't make that corner in his sleep.

My Odalisque

I tear down the curtains of my life
I rip apart the carpets of my life
I cut up the suits and shirts of my life
And then paste them on the ceiling
As if they belong there.

But still there is my odalisque
Stretched out sated on her mattress
In her dangerous red culottes
That blouse stitched from mist
Those breasts, arabesques.

I scrape down the walls of my life
I brick up the doors of my life
I strip off the bed and boards of my life
And hide her under the linen
As if she belongs there.

But still there is my odalisque
Napping like a cat in curl toed slippers
I know her face and body by heart
In that alphabet of longing
If I were a poet, I'd write poems in.

9 + 1 = Picasso

I

Fetch me the head of la belle Fernande.
Dampen the dirt. This knife has an edge.

Death shares my skin—she'll never leave me.
Clay is the dough I knead into bread.

Love is a feast. My blood will not rest.
I'll work the earth till it's dry in my hand,

Carve down the line so the line is made flesh,
My face in her face, this eye in that head.

II

Each time I make a love, I waste a love.
I burn the bridesmaid when I take the bride.

The sheets were white in the sanatorium,
Her lips blew red; roses bloomed inside.

I prised pins from her breast—oh, my pretty one—
Sweated her sweat the night she died.

Each time I waste a love, I make a love
To raise another bird into the sky.

III

When first I saw her dance, she was air—
The absence of everything I fear—

An empty hand, naked feet, her hair
A helmet to ward off the world.

I could not leave her there, I drew her near.
Now her madness stalks down my years

Stripped of all flesh, dressed up in furs
Like a mother rejected at birth.

IV

Art is the child of a man
And a mountain of men.

One day I left that charnel house
And swallowed the sky

And every cloud was a woman,
One woman, the shape of a cloud.

I saw a poem in her face
And told the story of the sun.

V

Dora was born weeping.
She's filled the seven oceans

And overflows her mourning
Through my hand in motion.

Live your last goodbyes
Like little deaths, nothing spoken.

My Dora is the sigh
Of defeat, for you, the broken.

VI

Blast my bugle. Summon the day.
Feed that fire and spin the wheel.

Love is a woman, lithe and full.
We break our fast on bread and milk

She serves in breast shaped bowls.
I bake clay in the valley of gold.

Beyond my oven, only the Lord,
And fading flamenco of her heels.

VII

The bed yawns its own hole.
Don't fall in this mouth. Please do.

So many drowned here before
You, Rapunzel, let down your braid

To haul me from this dark.
Remember how the room grew cold

The night the sky came crashing in,
A fork of lightning in my grasp.

VIII

Your age is all I crave, nothing more.
Shall we exchange, my gift for your youth?

Yes, wear your coat buttoned to the neck,
Your hair tied tight against the crown.

I like the way you look, then look away.
One day I'll make you twelve metres tall.

Forever, you'll look both ways at once,
Young and eager in New York.

IX

I saw you before we met, as is my way.
When I see an empty space, I smile.

See how the shadow penetrates?
I demand surrender. I am frail.

Let me lay my paint upon your face,
Break down its parts, then mend you

With nails, do the hard labour of art.
I fail to finish. There can be no end.

X

They say your face looks just like mine,
But I am a man of many disguises.

You are the bone behind the eye;
The space between us is closing.

I have willed all that you take.
I cannot sleep. Do not make me still.

Let me end my days as a child,
Painting the way a child paints.

The Empty Chair

Vincent inhabits Kyoto, I live in Arles.
We share a four room yellow house.

Where I part grain, he wades through rice
Crowned by a straw coned coolie hat

To scare crows with a five franc gun,
Spook boys with his scarecrow eyes.

I despise the madness of that hat,
His peasant smock, the candlelight

He paints me by side on, or worse—
When I'm not there—an empty room, an empty chair.

And when he sees his face in mine
He says: 'that's me, but me gone mad.'

And mad he went. And mad he is.
His colours baked mad in the sun.

He never saw a mountaintop
But worked up to the peak of one

Propped up his easel at its edge,
Took a razor to what only he could hear

Came down to earth with that severed ear,
Still hot to touch, the cut of meat

He washed and wrapped, laid on a plate
For a brothel girl to smell, to taste—

'Keep this and treasure it,' he said,
Mad with colour flowing from his head.

Bacon Dust

The thrill of sable
Before it's dipped
Becomes a bottle
That's launched its ship.
As my last seed
Is sown, I trust
You'll swallow a dose
Of Bacon dust.

It's such a con:
Just as I sussed
How an old man
Can deal with lust
Sleep lays down
Its finishing crust—
Label my bag
'Bacon dust'.

Unframe the windows
Unhinge the doors
Rollup the ceiling
Fold up the walls.
Here stood my body—
This is a bust.
Now hoover up
That Bacon dust.

The art connoisseur
Will say 'Vintage stuff!'
As he gets a nose
Of this fragrant muff,
Snort it like coke
Or sniff it like snuff,
A line or a pinch—
Pure Bacon dust.

My nerves are jarred,
Racked with paint
Between *Cardinal Red*
And *Crimson Lake*—
For a sanguine colour
Sharper than rust
Hand the man down
Some Bacon dust.

Reglaze the windows
Hang up the doors
Rollout the ceiling
Unfold the walls.
Museums are morgues,
Let's not discuss
The provenance of
My Bacon dust.

Unmarked Exit

Four in the morning, moon
walking—one eye cast out,
the other within—Jeanne

slips from her bad dream
backwards through a window frame
and into a notebook of sky

where she drew herself naked—
artist and model—or was drawn,
raw, out of her coconut skin;

split, spilt like milk, left
to sour on the Paris street,
a sardine stain on the sheets;

the scarlet pages of Modi's bed
where their slender hands were tied,
wrists thrice bound by marriage thread:

the cut cord freed a living child;
the living cord, a child unborn;
the golden cord, a chilling dawn.

Easel Hawk

Birdman regards manbird
Through a squint of sky;
Peers down the barrel
Of his beaky, beady eye;
Preens back his feather cut
With a taloned hand;
Plucks bird self right down
To the down of a man.

Manbird regards birdman,
Scrapes his claw on board;
Scours and grouts pigments
Like a smithy forges swords;
Hangs fresh from its frame,
Till it sags in flabby folds,
Bends his bones; knows death
Is not the end of growing old.

Birdman regards manbird,
He's seen our kind before;
He loiters in the window,
You shiver at the door—
He welcomes all his victims
As a hawk picks out its prey,
And you are that small animal
Left on his mat today.

An Artist of Whom Nothing Is Known

I

In an upstairs room on Moonlight Street
His Majesty of Cats, a tabby tweed,
laps his brush in a palette of cream

lays glaze on the pearly thigh
of a girl who lolls like a tongue
in the chaise longue of his mouth:

drinks in youth till his lips are damp;
clamps a cigarette in the crack;
breathes in, leaving a phallus of ash.

II

He is as old as the century,
hangs his skin on a bent wire frame
wrapped in kimono silk brocade,

floats through the palace of a hundred rooms
rearranging flowers, a bowl of fruit—
each still life, life in slow decay;

each girl on the cusp a drawn out spring
that drifts into summer lethargy
and fades with hands and feet unmade.

III

He builds a scaffold of windows, climbs
out of this world, into the laudanum light
that crucifies shadows and tails our days

leaving Alice behind with her blank eyes.
She steps from the canvas into your sleep
and is dreamt, real as a hole in the face

knocked there by his hammering gaze.
When she whispers, her breath is a stain—
Never trust a man with only one name.

Bella, Bella

Your silence is mine. My eyes are yours.
The distance between us is ours.

The rooftops of Paris are singing.
I work through the blue light of dawn;

subsist on loaves and cured herring
to daub colour on cut-up shirts.

This is our floating world. We fly
amongst steeples between heaven and earth,

graze the meadows of flowers
and swathe rainbows on a canvas of cloud.

Still there are days when the curtains fall down.
This city grew from a village like ours:

I can hear cattle lowing, pluck
their tongues, brush shades of lament

with these lips that still bear the scent
of our first kiss. You are what I miss.

The sun is an intruder at the door.
I cover the mirror, shutter all windows,

turn my canvas to the wall; watch
the room grow dark before these eyes—

Still yours,

Marc.

Nip the Bud

There you are in my lidded eyes:
our flesh is shared and unalike
as meat and bone. I have pared
me of all excess and you, sister,
are doubled up with joy, blessed
to be me and me you, changelings
who swap bodies like siblings
cross-dressing in each other's skin.

I can take lines for a wicked walk
with my fingers, nibbed like quills;
smear on swabs of colour with
the pads of idle thumbs. Leave
quite a mess on sheets and soil
blankets smudgy red, patterned
with palm prints and hanks of hair.
Life is murder, my elder sister:

limpen limbs and rearrange
your rib cage like a ragman's doll.
Make button eyes and exchange
your face for my mask. Re-enact
our parents' honeymoon *tristesse*
in that Trieste railway hotel
where you were my splayed butterfly,
and I your skewering pin.

House of the Genius

I

Nested in a broken bay,
that legendary bird:

its feathers plucked away,
its viney flesh withered

to a crib of bleached out bones
that cradles nine empty wombs:

a staging place, now honed
of actors, props, costumes

to the unfinished canvas
of an unlived in room.

II

A ghost enters from the wings—
blood sweetening his pits—

to greet your day with laughter,
a geranium behind his ear.

Stinking like a goatherd, dressed
as a Moorish prince, he winks

at the moon rock where she skinned
her knees beneath the locust's belly

as he dared his head inside her
to taste how it feels to be condemned.

III

And the fisherman, as old
as she was then, told us

how the slave of that second bed
became mistress of the first

where, spread on his deck
purring like a Cadillac, she said:

A rabbit, skinned and stewed,
is a gift, or pigeon, well-plucked;

pets are loved to be killed,
and friends like you to be fucked.

The Cookbook Bible

Mother is arranged on her ebony chair,
a haunt of ink on the scumbled grey
of that plain spoken studio wall.
Her new world palette is flesh well set
on the bone of an old world shell
by his sauce of copal and turpentine.
She stares long, hard, through and beyond
the pane he bares to light up the stage;
their life is work and wiping away;
each holds an ice white square of lace
to catch a tear, a stray drop of paint.

Draw a thread from her knotty eyes
out through a chink in the etching frame:
follow its line down Chelsea streets
and sail the shanty to the brine.
Set your prow to Paris—raise a glass
of blood to art—let its dark chalice
spill wine on the white Russian plain.
Then bear starboard for the grey Atlantic
and ride the vast blankness of its waves
into the saving beyond of America
to bottle what you find at its heart.

Gas, 1940

He pumps the gas in miles,
gauges life that way. Oils
the last engine of the day. Wipes
the windshield of dead flies.
Inflates the tyres. Just right,
he says, tapping the bonnet
with his hand. Its crankshaft
turns—another customer done
and dusted. The forecourt clock
ticks over. He flips the sign
from open to closed, dims
the lights, and dusk comes in
from where the road merges
with a smothering of trees.

Not the yellow wood, its fork,
nor the birch wood, though that
is dark as dreams, but the wood
he converses with—his father
felled timber there, cleared
this lot, his son was snatched
from the fringe—a borderline
where man's conquest ends
and nature begins. A storm
marshalls all its winged forces
across the pond. He feels
a breeze, dunks his grimy hands.
His overalls need laundering—
he'll pound them clean tonight.

Warhol Triptych

Marilyn's Lips

Life is a series of images
that change as they repeat:

being born, being kidnapped;
fantasy love, reality love.

Death can really make you—
it would be very glamorous.

The movies make emotions—
when things happen, it's like watching TV.

Even beauties can be unattractive.
People look the most kissable

in low lights and trick mirrors:
putting bright colours on Marilyn's lips—

all over the spread, under the pillow—
there was something special

about the way she moved her head;
my un-cut-out cut-out doll.

That's a real person with those mannequins.
I think everybody should be a machine.

Don't pay any attention
to what they write about you;

just look at the surface, there's nothing behind.
It's hard to be your own script,

just measure it in inches;
the machinery is always going.

Liz 13

I love Los Angeles. I love Hollywood.
I believe in plastic surgery

that people don't need to have.
But I love plastic. I want to be plastic

and then sold into slavery.
I can't say anything about it.

I'm not prepared for it.
I am a deeply superficial person.

I have social disease:
I have to go out every night

stuffed into a shopping bag
on Elizabeth Taylor's finger.

Liz Taylor knows this.
I think everyone should be bugged

all the time. I'm so empty
I masturbate to Duran Duran.

I would really like to vacuum the Vatican,
be reincarnated as a great big ring.

Look at the surface of me, there I am.
It's too hard to look in the mirror.

Automation is a way of making things easy.
Buying is more American than thinking.

A coke is a coke. Liz Taylor drinks coke.
All cokes are the same. All cokes are good.

Jackie OK

I like to watch daytime TV at night.
I was painting in my studio—

scared of the dark, scared of the light—
heard the news over the radio,

the words that made cops cry:
the mosquito is the state bird of New Jersey.

You just couldn't get away from the thing—
I don't think I missed a stroke.

I'm so empty I just can't think;
tell me the words, they'll come out of my mouth.

Love is not sweeping the nation.
It's something that you see all the time:

TV and radio, programming everybody to be sad.
You're not around to know what's happened.

The first wish is to be able to wish,
little stars that just flicker away.

I am making a movie about sleep:
people who just walk into other people.

My words are coming from behind me.
Somebody just walks in and takes over.

I never think that people die—
they just go to department stores.

Department stores are the new museums—
they sell all the paintings off the walls.

Found Lost Sign

You cannot lose a cat
As you can lose a mind—
They just go missing, forget themselves,
End up in some other paradise
Eating from the wrong bowl.

I wrote a poem, a sign
That announced the loss of my mind
To the nation, hoping to entice
That stray back through the flap
It made its escape from.

I offered a reward, a token
Of heart-felt appreciation;
That tiger in my tank
Frantic alone in its cage
Was willing to give blood.

I chose to portray my mind
As a brain fruit, large and grey
Like a food designed for elephants,
And scribed the name—my name—
It would answer to when sober.

I posted that sign on pillar-boxes
And mailed it to those phone booths
That serve as 3-D contact magazines
From which it was pilfered
By those collectors of my work

Who have never known the trauma
Of losing their only cat
Or their other, occasional mind—
The one that writes poems
And finds lost signs.

The Man Who Ate Himself

It began with rituals of scarification.
He inked pictograms beneath his skin.
Made a stud cushion of his own scrotum.
Endured to enjoy. Had steel chains link
His to her nipples, her lips to his tip.
Made love on blood soaked rubber sheets
As her ringed hood hooked his Prince Albert prick.
So much was sour till pain made it sweet.

The first cut: he made an amputee.
Played piggy with his fingers. Got the taste.
Hacked a pound of flesh from his right thigh—
A self-basting roast; he wanted no waste.
Limbs were sacrificed. He ordered a trolley.
Non-vital organs became chow mein.
Senses waned. Life continued. Impulsively.
Till the trunk, mouth to arse, was all that remained.

He regarded the groin with his one seeing eye,
Licked his chops and began to contort:
For the hanging judge, a bloody assize!
He said, self-swallowing as one would a sword.
There was little of him that proved inedible—
But for some offal he'd left on the shelf,
A wig of hair, spare teeth, chewed-up nails—
By the Devil and Christ he ate himself.

The Larkin Lads

Wear wings of jazz
on boots recast in lead:

have one top hat,
a nest for two egg heads

and magic wands
that double up as sticks;

time's grey magicians
up to their old tricks . . .

Shuffle with a shrinking pack.
Stuff a rabbit into cats.

Saw young girls until they blur.
Take a hammer. Make it tap

beats out on a pocket watch.
Hear it tick. Hear it tock.

Lend no mind to conjuring
bones out of the magic box

we all end up sleeping in.
Even the Larkin Lads

who'll close the show in socks
to the hottest licks of jazz.

Old Iron

Old Iron set sail for Labrador
In a navvy's cauldron coracle

The sunburnt moor of Zennor
The last flag of shore he saw.

On his tod against the waves
To bank the world's last cod

Where the sprats are overflowing
And the magpies out of range.

Best out of it, see. Better the brine
Than a pit without a stone—

The rag'n'bone is full now
And all his paint pots empty

After fifteen years behind the brush
And a century at sea,

As a cloud that's barely baby sized
Crawls across the pink-blue sky

And the milky teat of sun
Is sucked dry and put away.

The Rothko Room

Man once walked in space
There's dark behind that door
Hooked by an umbilical
To Earth, your lover's face
At dawn—a madrigal
We rise and then we fall
Are candles now, not stars

> *There's a rumour*
> *Of a tumour*
> *In the Rothko room.*

If this army's on the march
We forgot to lace our boots
Stamp that dirt down hard, boys
Good men died for you
Eyes right, and then salute
The old guard wrapped in scarves
Wound round their scarlet suits

> *There is womb blood*
> *In the wound blood*
> *Of the Rothko room.*

Roll aside the stone
These palms have bled for wood
Did the Marys do their work?
Those scars have yet to bind
The guards? So drunk, they're blind
The healer's not at home—
I'd wake him if I could

> *There is moonlight*
> *In the tomb light*
> *Of the Rothko room.*

Return to Kalighat

Darshan with Dalai Lama

I am here to kill the Dalai Lama.

I'll greet him as a fellow horologist,
show him my silver pocket watch
and tell him his time is up.

Or strangle him with this white scarf
before his kung fu monks can chop me down,
and that will end the movie of his life.

And if he has his Nobel Prize about his person,
I will beat his person with it most viciously,
and hope his bones rest in peace.

Should he offer me a knotted prayer string
I'll use it as a garrotte to finish him off
and bring an end to his suffering.

They told me, if I ever meet a Buddha
on the road, I must kill him. He is the first
and the last I'll ever meet.

I am here to kill the Dalai Lama.

Everest

Mountains rise to cradle snow,
the young upstarts of the world
not yet beaten back to earth
by the spanking of monsoons.
Scan the range from Tiger Hill
on a day dry-cleaned by dawn;
take yourself on a three week walk

through the cloud trees of Sikkim;
cross the bones of Shangri-La,
and there, beyond the five-peaked fist,
is Everest from where the lord
who rules them all sighs *climb this*
into the ears of mountaineers,
and who are they to deny him?

Now train your deepest lens
a haul from flagpole's highest reach
and if you know your flesh from snow
you'll spy young Mallory there,
carved from marble where he fell
eight decades since, five layers
of wool whipped off him, clawing air.

Three times he came—a sacrifice
of toes and then a life—not defined
by what the summit baggers claim
now in a yomp from camp to camp,
tethered to their leathery guides
whose brows ripple with the frowns
of two continents colliding.

High Water Down

Follow the river, the ice melt
Rises each pale afternoon
Till mountains fall to their knees,
Necks to the blade of the moon.

Weave through those trees by the water,
Their leaves float leagues to the sea
Whose raindrops cannot remember
Why they cried to be free.

And the sea itself is uncertain
How it began at the peak
Where snowflakes soft as ashes
Are all that the sky has to speak.

Fishing in Orissa

The fishermen
are bent over us
in fascination
at all of the technologies
of clever fishing.

We Englishmen
are waiting
in anticipation
of seeing the
simplicities
of clever fishing.

The fish
are swimming
in the ocean
eating other fish.

The ocean waves
back and forth
keeping its own time.

And time?
I don't suppose time
cares how long it takes.

The Snow Leopard

'Have you seen the snow leopard?
No! Isn't that wonderful?'
—Peter Matthiessen

I spy seeker in the valley below:
he pads through snow in goat skin boots,
a flock of cloud above his head
herded by the white-toothed winds.

I am here and there where he is not:
rubbing cheek on bark, in stalking stance,
belly down behind that cairn of rocks,
topped with rags on sticks.

He scans the crest with me in mind
but human vision is not trained
to give to ice its many names
or distinguish shades of white

so I leave a trail of tell tale signs:
scat and scrape, the gutless gorge
of stray blue sheep, picked bone clean
by a whirlwind of black winged choughs.

He wanders above the timberline
of bare and stunted cypress trees
bothering his god with flags and stones
to dare these crystal mountain tops,

his trail as strong as yak butter tea,
until he tips over the horizon's ledge
stripped of all thought but his belief
that one day seeker will spy me.

Grey, Languorous

The old monkey of the mountains
sits in his Bodhi tree
tail plumb as the pendulum
of a cobwebbed grandfather clock.

He's given up on the world—
all of its comforts, all of its vices—
left his home, abandoned the tribe,
renounced his daughters, rejected those wives,
relinquished his sons. His work is done
and he has done with it.

He seeks the enlightenment
that comes to those who wait.
And wait. And wait alone.

But your passing by has touched him
with an awareness of an awareness—
what if he's missed out on life's pleasures
only to retain the sum of its pains?

Face rubbed down with coal,
eyes glowing in their grates,
he hates the world that found him
out while he was searching.

Screech loud as an Eagle Owl's,
star-shaped as he leaps—
he would surely crush the skull
of any monk who wandered by
on his own path into the mountains.

Tusker

The old rogue was here an hour ago:
came crashing through the matchwood trees,
stopped our toy train in its tracks,
then forged on through Darjeeling leaves
in search of moonshine and weed.

If he had a mahout, he'd tossed him
as a gumboot buffalo might flick
a tick-picking egret from his hide,
tipped his trunk and bellowed a cry
buoyed up on a full tank of steam.

The elephant men were on his trail
armed with knockout darts and chains—
it takes quite a spike to pierce that hide.
They'd lost their drink, he'd lost his mind,
bloodhound eyes rolling in his head—

a kingdom conquered, then occupied
by the urge to lose, lose it again.
No stash is safe, however contained—
his sense of smell now rice wine primed,
his liver moaning, day and night.

They find him sleeping, vast and grey
as a monument carved from rock.
He dreams of drinking, as drunkards do.
The mountains tremble with his snores.
They cock their guns. Give him a shot.

Keena of Nandankanan

Her cubs pace crazed circles:
lose themselves in the caged pad
of muffled claw on concrete:
react to the beating of bars
with roars that might be yawns.

Trace back monsoons: orbits
on the banyan tree Keena drifts
beneath have shrivelled away,
as dark slashes on her pelt
stage shadow plays in the grass.

She flares her nostrils to the breeze;
snags at the forest's asphalt edge;
wary as a stalker, yet driven,
not by hunger, but something deeper—
a stirring of the brood in her blood.

Scent waves beat strange drums
in her skull; draw her far into
this human kingdom
but she is guided by the lure
of pheromones, nature's telegraph.

Tooth and claw alone could sort
menagerie into prey and predator
but she slinks past each meaty prize,
her nearly-lover waiting across the divide
of mortar, rail, moat water and razor wire.

He raises himself to the night sky,
jaws parting like a mantrap
as her orange flare blazes into his;
eyes Catherine Wheels, they begin
their pounding lullabies, never to go back.

A Cow Is Dying

Beneath the house of the poet Tulsi
where Ganga mud meets Chunar stone
a cow is dying.

Sheltered under saffron
cosseted beneath a blanket
with fires burning at head and feet
a cow is dying.

Back beaten, legs broken
a cow is dying
and children bring her garlands,
while a sadhu ladles water
onto her lolling tongue.

A cow is dying,
her eyes two balls of crystal
cloudy and mysterious with pain.

A raga is played in mourning
today is the day it speaks of—
a cow is dying

Beside an upturned rowboat
a cow is dying
and when darkness falls
like a great black bird

She will be dipped into the river
tenderly as the bathing of a calf,
a mother swallowing her own milk.

The Indian Museum

We enter from the jam of Chowinghee, where striking bankers chant softly for a pension worthy of their well-groomed moustaches.

Pass through the sniff of security and climb the marble staircase on your left, avoiding the greetings of pigeons that fly through the nets provided there for their safety.

Observe for a moment as an inefficiency of sweepers rearrange dust while babus of uncertain education and no purposeful employment perspire over yesterday's papers.

Now enter the Zoological Gallery through its second door, tall enough for a mastodon to walk through. Avoid the mastodon.

Admire the mahogany and glass certainties of the Age of Discovery, the ordering of all things dead or never alive. Your ancestors expired for this Empire of Knowledge.

Overhead, a squadron of free-hanging fans will remind you of the Blitz. If rocks and bears amuse you, you'll feel at home. But if the bears throw rocks, you are advised to feed them.

Do not stray in too far. Look left, and there, bathing in a bell jar of formaldehyde, is my only child, preserved pre-birth but full-term.

If the nuns I pay to pray for him are there, kneel down besides them and cross yourself. See how they move their lips without speaking, as if God is a lip reader. God is a lip reader, so follow their lead.

You will see that my boy is not lonely, his familiars comfort him: the eight-legged goat, the two-bodied calf, and the one-eyed dog. And now you have joined them. Say hello for me.

Relics

The habit wears her scent,
takes her shape, almost stands
where it drapes, hem frayed
by the street's uneven scrape,
homespun worn to a single ply
gathered pleating at the knees
where she knelt to pray, scrubbing
a shit-hole with ashes and twigs
each Godless, God-blessed Sunday.

Albanian leather, Bengali stitched—
the nun skin of her hands and feet
calloused by the work, no task
too small for her tiny frame,
riddled with nails and thorns.

Life is brief as an eye can blink:
now she cowers in her vast tomb,
where flowers spell out her name
and candles faintly glow. Her child-
sized room remains unchanged—
high chair, short bed, school desk—
great life reduced to a pencil case—
eraser and blade, wood-bound lead
she wrote her last words with.

The Great British Cemetery

Whenever, wherever I travel, I first ask the locals where the British are buried. They direct me there with invariable enthusiasm.

In Malaga we were committed vertically and beyond the shoreline as befits heathens. When land was reclaimed from the sea, they granted us a patch of it and there we lie, sunning ourselves.

In McLeod Ganj the graveyard is more Scottish than any in Scotland; the mountains higher, the tombstones more austere; only the diseases were foreign.

Elsewhere our war graves are well tended, whether we died as heroes or villains. We have killed and been killed all over the world.

But our greatest triumph is Calcutta where we took the funerary arts to new heights, its pyramids and columns rivalling those of classical Egypt or Greece, its urns stuffed with stories.

Some went to rest with children still eggs inside them, others with children beside them, ten in a dozen, baptised by fever or dead in childbed.

Barely off the boat, they flared up and fizzled away like Diwali fireworks, their youth a festival of light in the darkness.

A hundred servants to each family, one for each bodily function; now only the jackdaws and pariah dogs attend them.

And then abandoned to the disorder of history: a thieves' kitchen, stashed with Naxalite rifles, moonshine brewing beneath the weathered domes of Lieutenant Generals.

Such degradations are preferable to preservation somehow. I will end my days camped among graves, the tapping on my shoulder almost a relief.

The Ear Cleaner

Turban milky blue, like sky stirred.
Robes hang from a winning smile
with tools tucked in each pocket
last sterile as ingots,
spokes sharpened, tweezers ready—
the auricular sorcerer.

He carries a book of poetry—
testimonies mistranslated, ill-written
lies so bad they transcend
the truth, transmute into art.
He is irresistible, tiger-eyed.

See! he commands. Enough scum
to coat a coin is smudged on his thumb.
Dirty! Tut! Dirty! That's where
verbal diarrhoea collects then,
in the U-bend of the ear.

My syringe-toting grandmother
interrupts the delicate procedure
with a long-distance call
from another, more hygienic era,
sucks the dark stuff away.

For a day the world is improved.
Music of Delhi and Connaught Circus sound
so much clearer than muffled England.
Then the ear is sick like a baby.
Pus dribbles, the consistency
of sour milk.

The Shambler

Puzzled by the length of his skin:
I saw a lensman circle in orbit,
its beak shutter clicking, clicking

at a man who could part the Ganges
with a wave of his elephantine hand,
sagging like a trunk from his shoulder.

Lepers skate their karts from his path.
Beggars scrape up their coins and run.
The fingers of snake charmers freeze.
Cripples are cured by the sight of him.

He walks through streets so thick
with hair, lice can skip, head to head,
street to street, right across the town
and yet there is a moon of space about him,
a shifting crescent in his wake.

Too horrible even for charity to reach:
his skin is black and puffy, welted
and ripped: his eyes are menstrual—
he sees as far as his finger stalks.

Each limb heavy as a cross; lymphs blocked
by nematodes; arms outstretched from crutches
but empty of alms—he has grown up to be
a one-man caste; the true untouchable.

I once saw a horror film: people laughed
and screamed. I would like to have seen
The Shambler fall into that velvet hall,
crash through the screen, landing close,
close enough to steam up our 3D visors.

I would have that man strip himself clean
of latex and rags, a distressing disguise
unmasked. Welcome him as your guest.
His hands are strong hands, healing.

The Duchess of Kalighat

The 'Duchess' is a deranged butterfly:
his hair oiled and preened into an unwieldy bun
decorated with jasmine flowers. All the colours
of earth and sky are sewn into his sari,
his face a bloodied powder puff, as he flits
from car to car, rubbing his bodice-busting body
provocatively on the hot bonnets of Marutis
or pressing vermilion lips against the windscreens
of Ambassadors, his throaty voice hooting louder
than all the baying horns around him.

He is the star of every traffic jam:
crooning like Marlene Dietrich, a pouting crone,
handbag swinging like a mace; no one gets in his way.
One shake of his padded hips, his plumped out breasts
and the drivers forgive. He is of the third sex;
his maleness was bound by a cord and cut,
left to bleed dry then poulticed by the sisterhood,
dressed, anointed and scented with musks.

Barely a child, he was never a man,
became her, deserted father and mother
to make a living dancing and singing
new babies into the world—a good purse
or be cursed, end up with another changeling daughter.

At other times she trawls the bazaar
threatening to show off what is missing,
what has been gained, available to real men
at a realistic price. Queen of all vice,
she blesses the streets with gaiety,
sleeps in her own bed—velvet and lace,
silk draped; all things feminine.

But when the ambulance passes her way
she shrieks, stubs her long-holdered cigarette,
and, bowing, waves it by. The sisters inside
are saried in white homespun, blue bordered.
She calls them 'the moths' but they tend
even her kind. She offers them his respect.

Holi at Nirmal Hriday

My face is painted green
on Holi, my clothes scarlet
as a Marxist wildcat
looking for a strike to join.

At the drop of a wallet
you've got a march:
columns of banner waving ants
ripping mandibles of concrete
from the steel-framed jungle.

'Justice! Not charity!'
they chant: all male voices;
young and belching brimstone,
spraying statues with symbols and slogans—
red as my hair. The city is on fire.

The bus is a pressure cooker
on wheels, boiling passengers,
spitting them onto pavement slabs
like gobs of paan—to Nirmal Hriday,
Place of Pure Heart.
You could say I am a pilgrim.

I smell goat blood in the air:
bandicoots rummage in the rubbish dump
like cats after boggle-eyed mice:
House of the Dying—living like nowhere else.

Inside, beds crammed so close
they could share one giant mattress.
Queues always outside, and the streets:
efficient engines of replacement;
production lines that never stop.

Just drops in the ocean, sister,
Just band-aids and placebos.
Smiles of the vanquished don't always
bring joy to my heart—sometimes despair.

The ocean is made of drops, she says.
For a moment I unlearn my politics,
see a man empty his lungs onto his bed,
kneel beside him and rub his chest.

This Little Piggy Has None

Unpeeling the muslin parcel:
a butcher's joint, sawn
and cut by apprentice blade.

Pictures curdle the eye
more than the real can;
involvement making liquid
what would sour as pus
and solidify—an angry sty
on shock's freeze-frame.

The foot is half-formed
like a chinawoman's stump,
but unskinned and open.

Muscle fibres twitch, alive,
and only a second glance
reveals what feeds between,
plumping to fill the spaces
like new toes erupting
in place of those lost.

I hold the plastic pan
while thin chopstick fingers
pick out maggots like prawns.

They are foetal in perfection:
tiny abortions, beak-plucked
from their scarlet nest,
ready to emerge hungry-eyed,
black out of white, as flies.

How can I respond to
the confusion of a smile
that hovers across his face
while his gummy mouth
opens and shuts
as if miming last goodbyes.

One Irish Rover

Your brogue as broad as the Irish Channel,
you wore a wooden cross and cursed
with smiles dancing on your face.
Crying never cured a body,
laughter sang from the guts of yours.

Those Dublin eyes could stun any girl
across the span of a hurling pitch:
hair dark as Guinness, complexion creamy:
strong hands gently stripping the skin
from fruit so as to keep all the flesh.

India is a nation of recyclers;
at the rubbish dump we saw our scraps—
clotted with dressings and expectorations—
sifted, sorted and put to fresh use
in the feeding troughs of beasts and men.

A shrug of broad shoulders: trash cans
balanced on bamboo poles: we were milkmaids
from County Clare, gossiping the walking minutes away
and then silent at the door; a recollection
of true purpose and a strengthening of resolve.
If you see the shit first—clean it up.

That's what I call philosophy—first-hand.
You juggled oranges as you handed them out,
knew the common language of the body:
held men in your arms, sang *Carrickfergus*
in the soft tones of a native lullaby.

New Life in Hospice

We found a rats' nest:
stirring balls of pink baldness,
glued eyes still blind as pennies.

We'd chased their mother's tail:
scuttled her to their den and then,
scurrying, away again:
discovering in the food-store
her brood—their tiny breaths.

We wrap them in newspaper:
pass round the wards
a parcel of pulsing pleasure.

Smiles bare stumpy teeth,
bony fingers stroking gentleness.
Thin lips coo forgotten sutras:
bushels fall from their eyes,
igniting them—something heaven-sent.

I tie the bundle,
carry it outside,
grind it to the dust.

The colour of this page is red,
Ganesha's miniature vehicles dead—
even vermin are sacred
to the dying.

Duncan

A dinner plate sore
curves in his back
red deep down to porcelain bone
and elsewhere
flesh mats have opened
like the marks of scalding cups.

He is dressed
like a pop art table, grotesque
as a man half-carved
on the spit,
or some other terrible,
some wretched piece.

Pipes snake his outsides
giving him post-modem design;
somehow he is functional,
somehow he lives.

Art is a parody of suffering:
its greedy red fist
opening and closing
in mimicry of the heart,
Pain written on its palm.

Yet *pain* is a word he uses
generously; little white boys
dancing round his bed
like Morris men on amphetamines
administering to his every need
as if they are unique
in a ward full of hurt.

Ward 9

On the neon wall
my bellows are depicted
holed with rot,
as delicate as frayed leather.
Destiny is mapped in a shatter of stars
that cluster in the shadows.

In the sealed jar
my guests are breeding
slowly as they like: they have a life
at their mercy, multiplying
into the world at their leisure,
in search of new hosts to squat.

On the graphic chart
the mountains and valleys of fever
define a crazed landscape,
populated with mirages
of recovery and oases
of healing—drugs and disease on one sheet.

In my morning pot
orange gobs of sun,
pearls prized from the depths of science,
and sugar-coated manna balls
rattle like a baby's toy
or the triumph of an old man's rasp.

On my bony back
a bale's weight, a tiredness
that has leeched the flesh off me.
My breathing sounds like a car
failing to start. A February morning,
fog closing in. But just beyond—
Spring.

Delta Blues

The sun wheels, pulsing plasma balls.
The air tastes of pollen, not medicine.
Hay fever sneezes seize me, innocent
as grass, my rabbit eyes rheumy.

I have perfected a jelly-mould walk,
grown a scrub of beard to disguise
the blue delta of veins breaking through
the cellophane skin of my face.

A cabinet of pills rattle my pockets,
gullet, guts—depth charges of science
cross-haired on the foreign invaders,
unleashing untold funerals in my lungs.

Brother! O Brother! Those first words
tear at the muslin round my mind.
Brother! O Brother! A man lays into my arms.
As water slides from him, little is left.

His skin is raw. I want to cover it up:
struggle with shirt buttons, his dhoti knot.
He grasps the blanket as a comfort,
slumbers as his head strikes the pillow.

Standing a moment. Catching breath. Wondering
at its case. Caravansaries and prefab wards:
places of healing come in all shapes and sizes;
the heart is a mansion of many chambers—

I want to know them all. Those first words:
Brother! O Brother! I can still hear them call.

Close Shave

Painting on thick skin
soap left to dry contracts
tight over bone, fills gaps
with the taste of his mother.
Today I could be her.
His lids flicker, then glue.

Bristle on bristle, the brush
tickles out chuckles
in a whooping, wheezy rush.
I cannot tell a grimace
from a grin these days,
can barely bare my own smile.

The blade rakes back growth—
there is little proof of life
left floating in the bowl, few
limp strands stuck to its sides.
I don't get the mirror out,
let him picture his better self.

Looking in the looking glass
each morning, I watch my face
stealing years from the grave.
I'm told hair grows three days
more than the rest of you;
think on that each time I shave.

Time and a Place

That was the time and this is the place
And that was the man and this is his face
And it has never launched the smallest boat
Nor asked a daughter to fetch her coat
And it never will now, like them in there
Who fill a space the men I knew shared.
And this is the hospice and that is its wall
Beyond is the temple. I don't hear the call
Of my God or their Goddess—no one's at home—
But kneel at the tree hung with word wrapped stones
Left by would-be mothers wishing on sons
Or should've-been husbands just wanting a wife—
Favours to be granted, curses undone—
Or any damned one of us pleading for life.

Before Poetry

Before poetry
a face looked on the water
and was unmoved.

Before poetry—
7 days
and 1001 nights
of waiting.

Before poetry
we were friends
with matter
and fact.

Before poetry
there was reason
without limit.

Before poetry
we had not met.

Before poetry
we kissed the same mouth
but with different words.

Before poetry
we were married:
our divorce
had rhythm and rhyme.

Before poetry
our children
were not found
in books.

Before poetry
we laughed more
but at the wrong things.

Before poetry
we cried less
and that was sad.

Before poetry
life went on
more-or-less
as afterwards.

www.ingramcontent.com/pod-product-compliance
Lightning Source LLC
Chambersburg PA
CBHW022158080426
42734CB00006B/494